Welcome

Date: _____

Green English Kids

Decorate with leaves, berries and flowers.

MY GREEN ENGLISH JOURNAL

My Green ID

Name: _____
Surname: _____
Age: _____
Birthday: _____
Address: _____
Tel. n. _____
Favourite colour: _____
Favourite animal: _____
Favourite flower: _____

Paste your photo here

Green English - Level A   © Copyright ELI 2006

Worksheet 1.1

Welcome

Date: _____
What's the weather like today? It's _____

Temperature
☐ Hot
☐ Warm
☐ Cold

Our Green English Logo

Look at the logo!

What colour is it?

It's _____, _____
and _____ .

What is it?

☐ It's a flower.

☐ It's a berry.

☐ It's a leaf.

Find a similar leaf in the garden. Draw it here. Decorate it.

What's inside the logo?

The U_I_N _A_K

Green English - Level A   © Copyright ELI 2006

Worksheet 1.2

Welcome

Date: _____
What's the weather like today? It's _____

Temperature
☐ Hot
☐ Warm
☐ Cold

Green English Keywords

✂ Cut outs: 🖍 paste the words and the numbers.

Green English - Level A   © Copyright ELI 2006

Worksheet 1.3

The Orchard

Date: _____
What's the weather like today? It's _____

Temperature
☐ Hot
☐ Warm
☐ Cold

Parts of a Tree

✏️ Draw a tree and match the words to the picture.

- Bark
- Trunk
- Branch
- Flower
- Fruit
- Leaves
- Roots

Green English - Level A   © Copyright ELI 2006

Worksheet 2.1

The Orchard

Date: _____
What's the weather like today? It's _____

Temperature
☐ Hot
☐ Warm
☐ Cold

My First Tree

✏️ Draw your tree.

Leaves:
Yes ☐
No ☐

Size
Big ☐   Small ☐

Flowers:
Yes ☐
No ☐

Colours:
_____
_____
_____

Fruit:
Yes ☐
No ☐

Touch it: **Smell it:**
It is nice 🙂 ☐   🙂 ☐
It is yucky 😝 ☐   😝 ☐

Green English - Level A   © Copyright ELI 2006   Worksheet 2.2

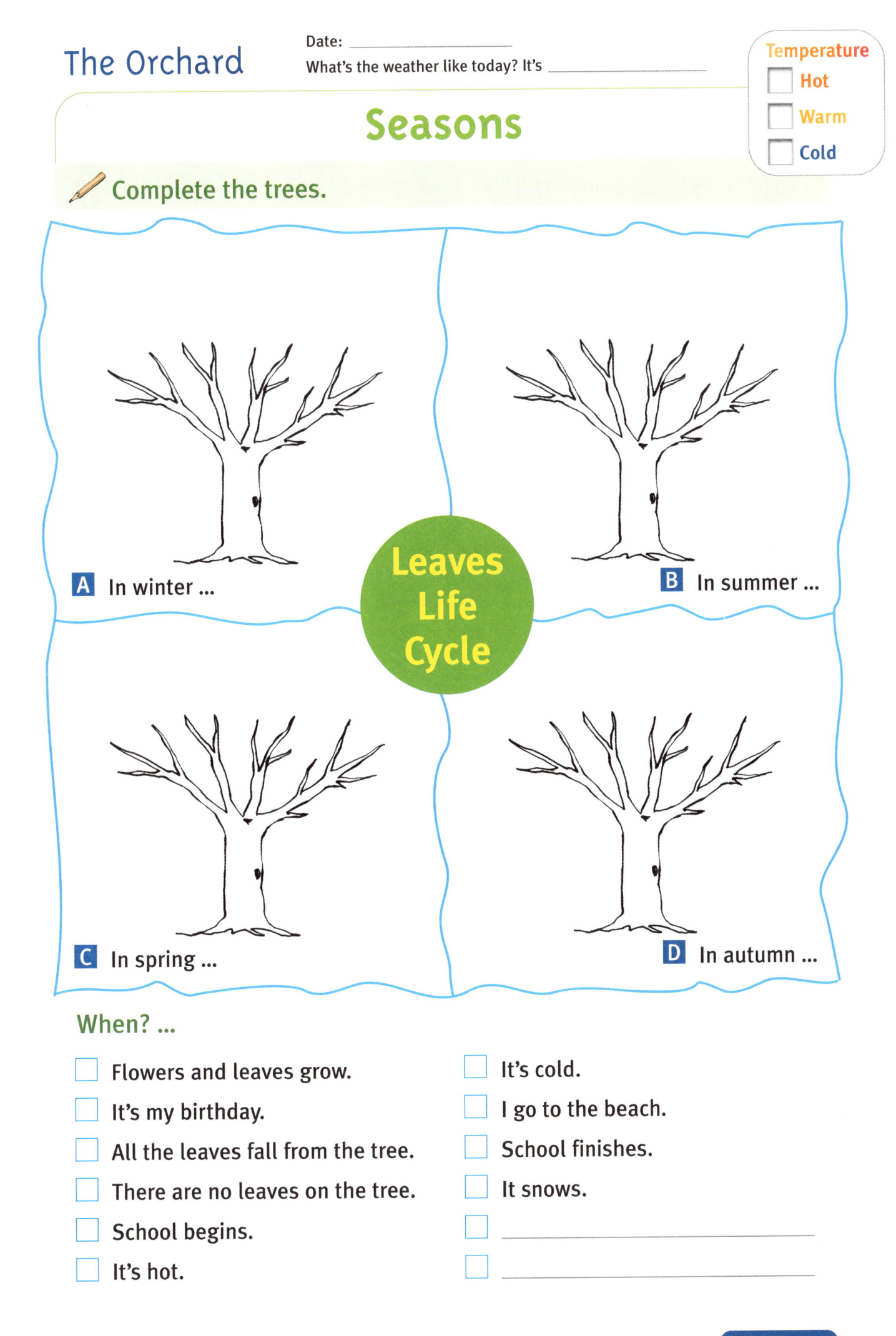

The Orchard

Date: _____
What's the weather like today? It's _____

Temperature
☐ Hot
☐ Warm
☐ Cold

Seasons

✏️ **Complete the trees.**

A In winter ...

B In summer ...

Leaves Life Cycle

C In spring ...

D In autumn ...

When? ...

☐ Flowers and leaves grow.
☐ It's my birthday.
☐ All the leaves fall from the tree.
☐ There are no leaves on the tree.
☐ School begins.
☐ It's hot.

☐ It's cold.
☐ I go to the beach.
☐ School finishes.
☐ It snows.
☐ _____
☐ _____

Green English - Level A   © Copyright ELI 2006   Worksheet 2.3

The Orchard

Date: _____
What's the weather like today? It's _____

Temperature
- [ ] Hot
- [ ] Warm
- [ ] Cold

Fruit

Do you like ...? 😊 Yes, I do. ☹ No, I don't.

APPLES _____

GRAPES _____

APRICOTS _____

PEACHES _____

ORANGES _____

PLUMS _____

BLACKBERRIES _____

STRAWBERRIES _____

CHERRIES _____

WATERMELONS _____

PEARS _____

MELONS _____

Green English - Level A   © Copyright ELI 2006

Worksheet 2.4

The Orchard

Date: _____
What's the weather like today? It's _____

Temperature
☐ Hot
☐ Warm
☐ Cold

Survey: What's your Favourite Fruit?

My favourite fruit is _____

#	Name	Fruit
1		
2		
3		
4		
5		
6		
7		
8		
9		
10		
11		
12		
13		
14		
15		
16		
17		
18		
19		
20		
21		
22		

The most popular fruit is _____

Green English - Level A   © Copyright ELI 2006

Worksheet 2.5

Plants

Date: _____
What's the weather like today? It's _____

Temperature
☐ Hot
☐ Warm
☐ Cold

Growing Things

✏️ **Draw. You need:**

a flower pot	soil	seeds	water

Complete with the keywords: seeds (2) , soil (3) , pot .

Fill the _____
with _____

Put the _____
in the _____

Cover the _____
with _____

Water it.

Choose, ✏️ draw and 🖊️ write. Your plants need:

CHOCOLATE   SUN   OIL   FRUIT JUICE   WATER   AIR

Green English - Level A   © Copyright ELI 2006   Worksheet 3.1

Plants

Date: _____
What's the weather like today? It's _____

Temperature
☐ Hot
☐ Warm
☐ Cold

Experiment: What do Plants Need?

✏️ **Draw. You need:**

5 small flower pots	soil	cress or bean seeds	a shoe box	water

Plant the seeds ...

1. Put one pot on the *window sill* and *water* it.

2. Put one pot on the *window sill* and *DON'T water it*.

3. Put one pot in a *shoe box* and *water it*.

4. Put one pot in the *fridge* and *water it*.

5. Put one pot in a *cupboard* and *water it*.

Observe.

Pot	after 3 days	after 5 days	after a week
1			
2			
3			
4			
5			

Green English - Level A   © Copyright ELI 2006

Worksheet 3.2

Plants

Date: _____
What's the weather like today? It's _____

Temperature
- ☐ Hot
- ☐ Warm
- ☐ Cold

Leaf Rubbing

✏️ **Draw. You need:**

paper	scissors	glue	leaves

Instructions:

Collect some leaves from the garden.

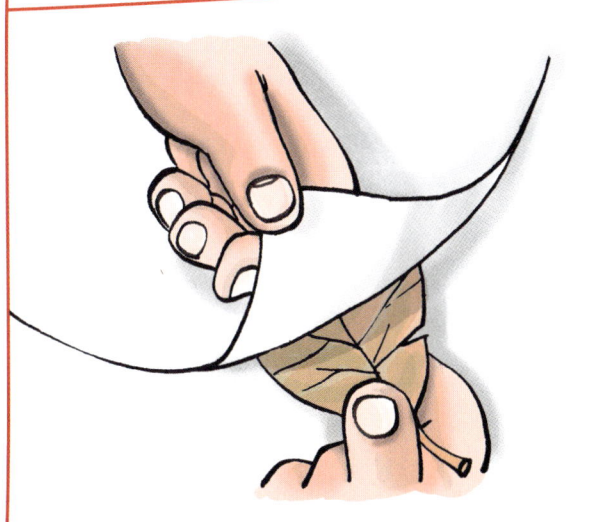

Put a leaf under a sheet of paper.

Gently rub the crayon all over the sheet of paper.

Cut out, label and use for decoration.

Green English - Level A © Copyright ELI 2006 FACT FILE 15 Worksheet 3.3

Plants

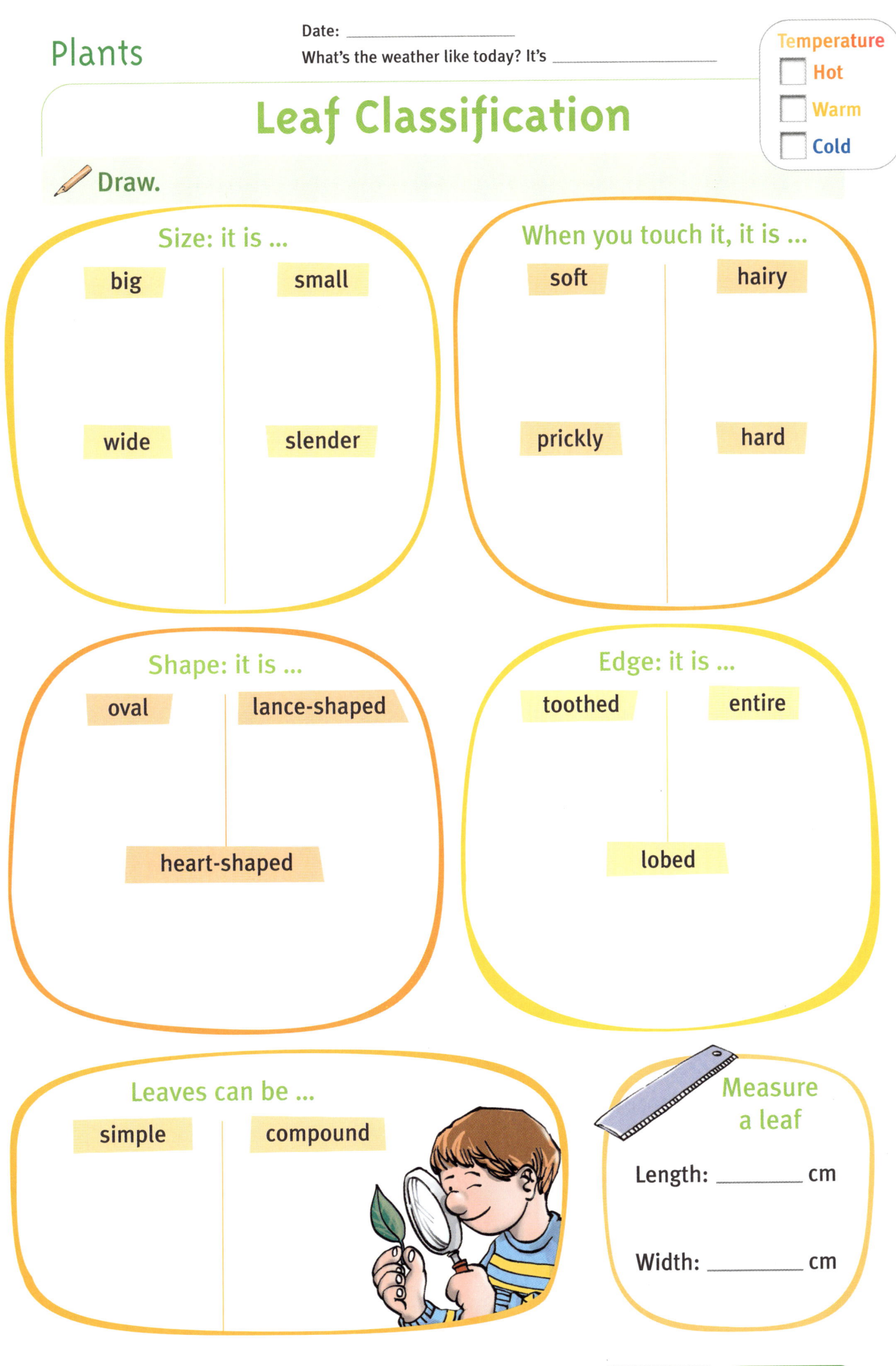

Date: _____
What's the weather like today? It's _____

Temperature
- [ ] Hot
- [ ] Warm
- [ ] Cold

Leaf Classification

✏️ **Draw.**

Size: it is ...
- big
- small
- wide
- slender

When you touch it, it is ...
- soft
- hairy
- prickly
- hard

Shape: it is ...
- oval
- lance-shaped
- heart-shaped

Edge: it is ...
- toothed
- entire
- lobed

Leaves can be ...
- simple
- compound

Measure a leaf

Length: _____ cm

Width: _____ cm

Green English - Level A   © Copyright ELI 2006   FACT FILE 16   Worksheet 3.4

The Three Rs

Date: _____
What's the weather like today? It's _____

Temperature
☐ Hot
☐ Warm
☐ Cold

Survey (1) What do you Recycle?

✏️ Colour the boxes.

I recycle	paper	plastic	glass	aluminium	organic waste
Name					
1					
2					
3					
4					
5					
6					
7					
8					
9					
10					
11					
12					
13					
14					
15					
16					
17					
18					

Green English - Level A © Copyright ELI 2006

Worksheet 4.1

The Three Rs

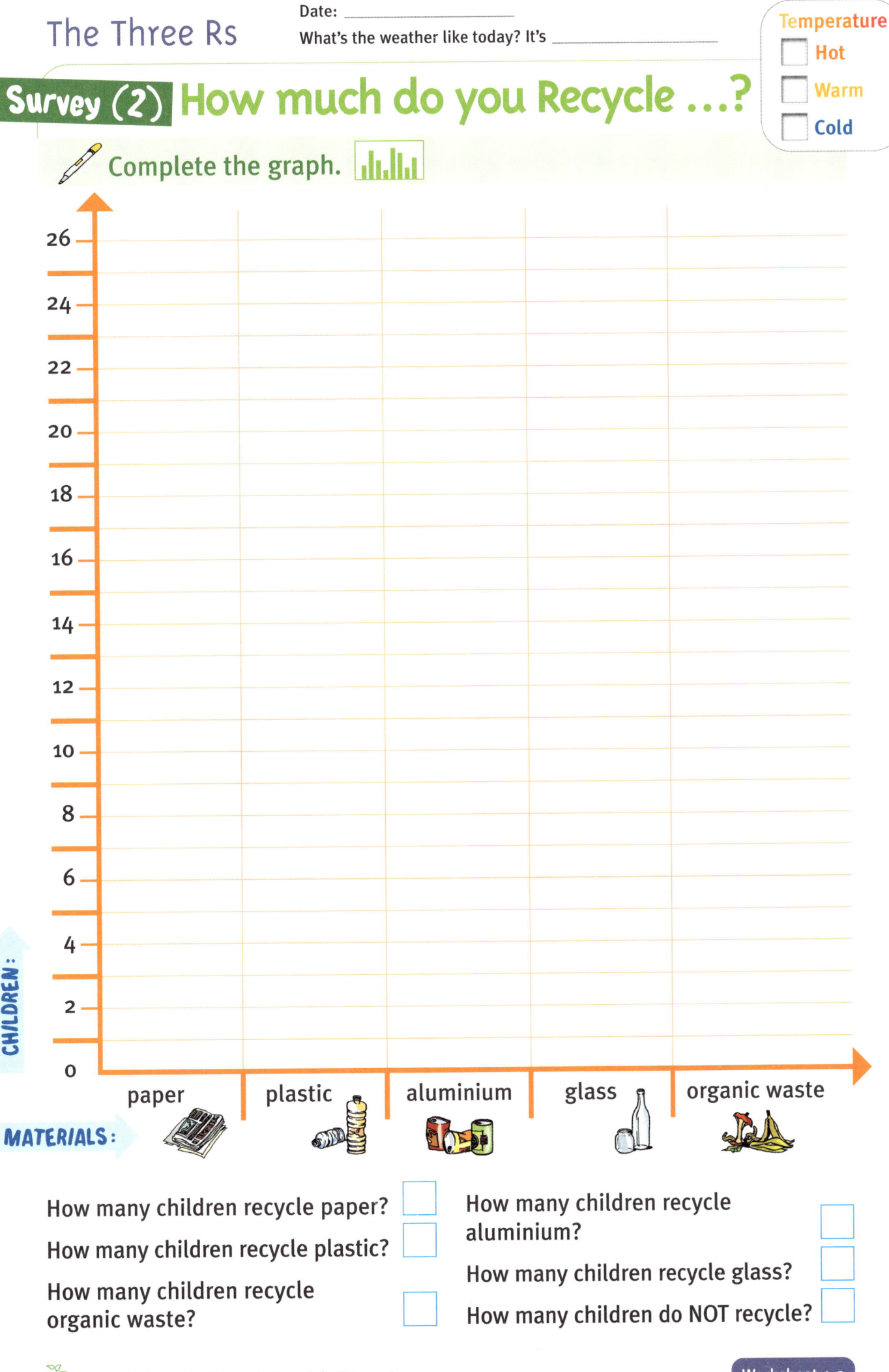

Date: _____
What's the weather like today? It's _____

Temperature
☐ Hot
☐ Warm
☐ Cold

Survey (2) How much do you Recycle …?

✏️ **Complete the graph.**

CHILDREN:
26, 24, 22, 20, 18, 16, 14, 12, 10, 8, 6, 4, 2, 0

MATERIALS: paper | plastic | aluminium | glass | organic waste

How many children recycle paper? ☐
How many children recycle plastic? ☐
How many children recycle organic waste? ☐
How many children recycle aluminium? ☐
How many children recycle glass? ☐
How many children do NOT recycle? ☐

Green English - Level A   © Copyright ELI 2006   Worksheet 4.2

The Three Rs

Date: _____
What's the weather like today? It's _____

Temperature
- [ ] Hot
- [ ] Warm
- [ ] Cold

Rubbish Bins

Complete the words and match the rubbish to the right bin.

P_AS__C

O_GA_I_ _AS__

_LU_I__UM

_A_E_

OTHER

_L_S_

Green English - Level A © Copyright ELI 2006

Worksheet 4.3

The Three Rs

Date: _____
What's the weather like today? It's _____

Temperature
☐ Hot
☐ Warm
☐ Cold

Reuse: Let's Make a Puppet

✏️ **Draw. You need:**

a plastic bottle with a top	cardboard	a piece of cloth	a stapler	sticky tape	wool	scissors

Complete the sentences and follow the instructions.
Keywords: head (2) , mouth , ears , arms , nose , legs , neck , eyes , top (2) , bottle .

1. Cut (✂) the _____ in three parts.

2. Make the _____ with the top and the bottom of the bottle.

3. Draw (✏) _____ , _____ , _____ and _____ on the cardboard.

4. Then cut out (✂) and stick on the head with sticky tape.

5. Stick the wool on the _____ with sticky tape.

6. Unscrew the _____ .

7. Put the cloth at the _____ of the bottle.

8. Screw the _____ on again.

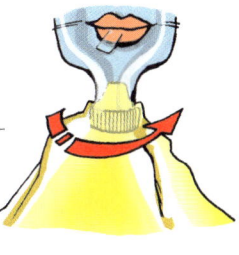

9. Staple the cloth.

10. Draw (✏) _____ and _____ on the cardboard. Cut out (✂) and fix to the cloth with the stapler.

Green English - Level A   © Copyright ELI 2006   Worksheet 4.4

The Three Rs

Date: _____
What's the weather like today? It's _____

Temperature
☐ Hot
☐ Warm
☐ Cold

Make your own Paper

✏️ **Draw. You need:**

paper	a bucket	water	a blender
a cloth	a plastic bowl	a clothes hanger with a nylon stocking	flowers, leaves, seeds

Draw the sun.

Green English - Level A   © Copyright ELI 2006

Worksheet 4.5

Water and Air

Date: _____
What's the weather like today? It's _____

Temperature
- ☐ Hot
- ☐ Warm
- ☐ Cold

Experiment: Soluble/Insoluble

✏️ **Draw. You need:**

| water | 5 spoons and 5 glasses | sugar | salt | oil | sand | stones |

Match:

1. ☐ Put the water in the glasses.
2. ☐ Put some sugar in a glass.
3. ☐ Put some oil in a glass.
4. ☐ Put some salt in a glass.
5. ☐ Put some sand in a glass.
6. ☐ Put the stones in a glass.
7. ☐ Stir and wait 4-5 minutes.

A, B, C, D, E, F, G

What can you see?

	yes	no
Oil disappears	☐	☐
Salt disappears	☐	☐
Sand disappears	☐	☐
Sugar disappears	☐	☐
Stones disappear	☐	☐

It disappears = it is **SOLUBLE**

It DOES NOT disappear = it is **INSOLUBLE**

Result:

SUGAR IS _____
OIL IS _____
SAND IS _____
SALT IS _____
STONES ARE _____

Green English - Level A   © Copyright ELI 2006

Worksheet 5.1

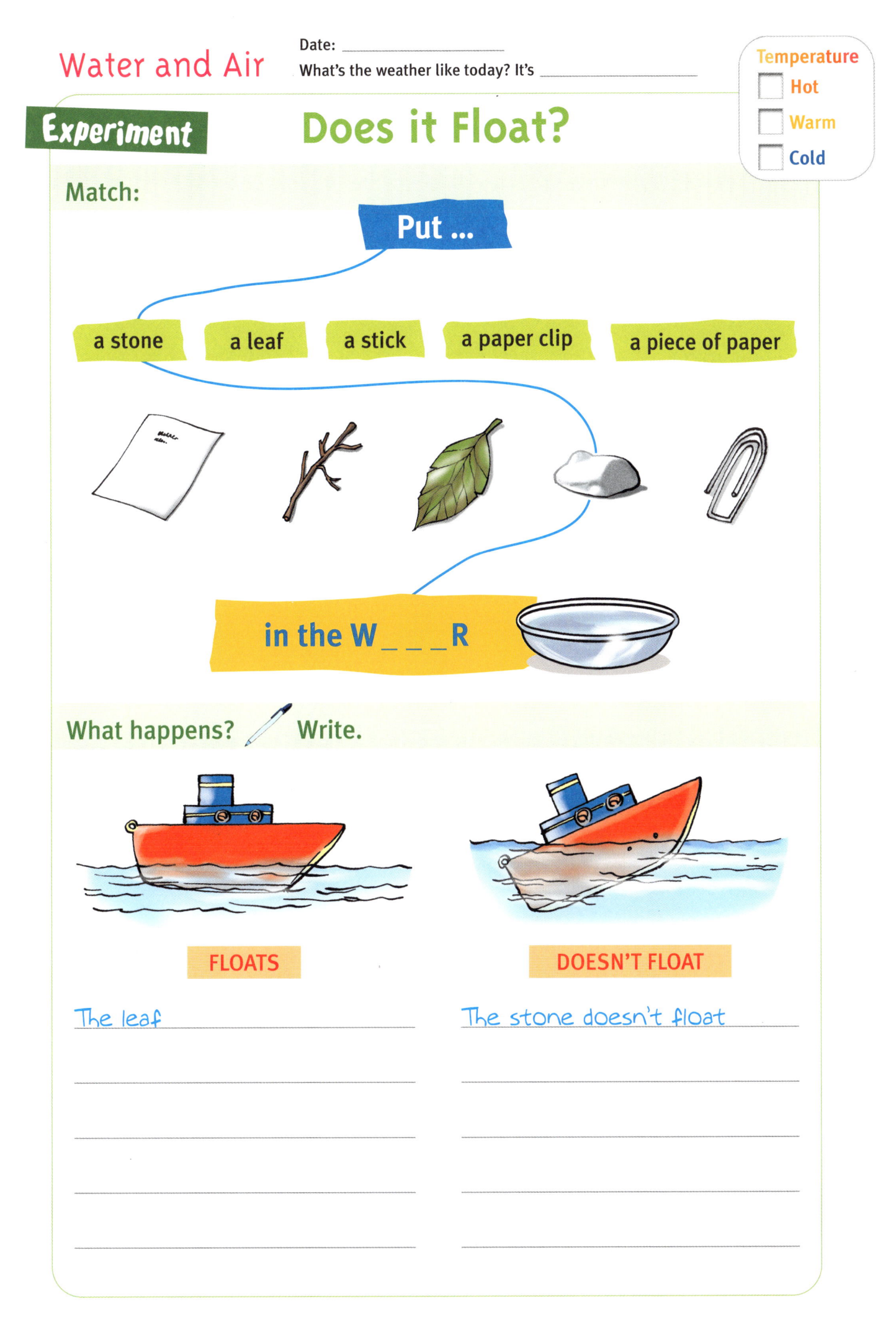

Water and Air

Date: _____
What's the weather like today? It's _____

Temperature
☐ Hot
☐ Warm
☐ Cold

Experiment: Does it Float?

Match:

Put ...

a stone · a leaf · a stick · a paper clip · a piece of paper

in the W _ _ _ R

What happens? Write.

FLOATS

The leaf _____

_____

_____

_____

DOESN'T FLOAT

The stone doesn't float

_____

_____

_____

Green English - Level A © Copyright ELI 2006

Worksheet 5.2

Water and Air

Date: _____
What's the weather like today? It's _____

Temperature
☐ Hot
☐ Warm
☐ Cold

A Story — Drip the Drop

Listen, read and ✏ draw the missing pictures.

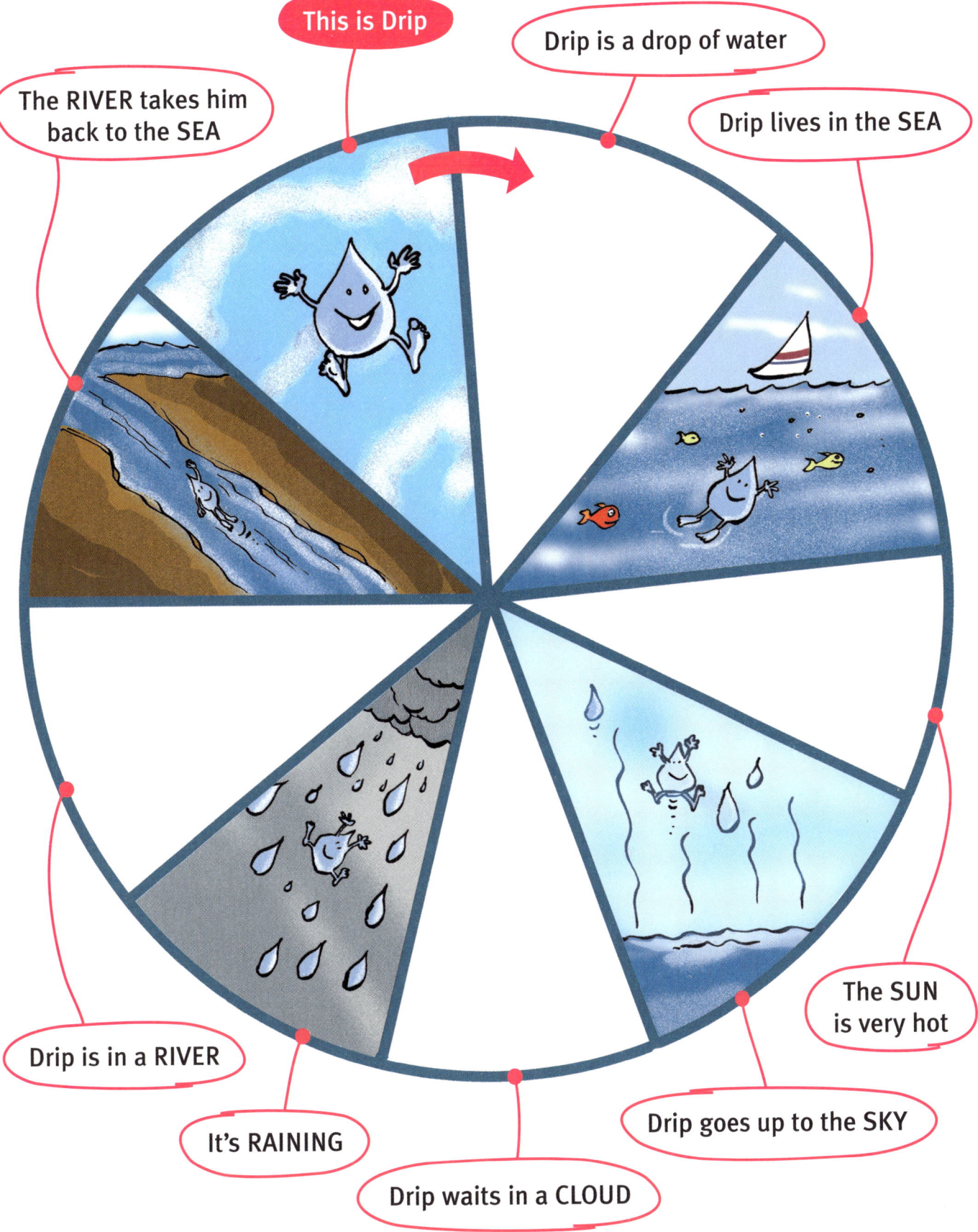

- This is Drip
- Drip is a drop of water
- Drip lives in the SEA
- The SUN is very hot
- Drip goes up to the SKY
- Drip waits in a CLOUD
- It's RAINING
- Drip is in a RIVER
- The RIVER takes him back to the SEA

Green English - Level A © Copyright ELI 2006

Worksheet 5.3

Water and Air

Date: _____
What's the weather like today? It's _____

Temperature
☐ Hot
☐ Warm
☐ Cold

Survey How do you Go to School?

Name	by bike	by bus	by car	on foot
1	☐	☐	☐	☐
2	☐	☐	☐	☐
3	☐	☐	☐	☐
4	☐	☐	☐	☐
5	☐	☐	☐	☐
6	☐	☐	☐	☐
7	☐	☐	☐	☐
8	☐	☐	☐	☐
9	☐	☐	☐	☐
10	☐	☐	☐	☐
11	☐	☐	☐	☐
12	☐	☐	☐	☐
13	☐	☐	☐	☐
14	☐	☐	☐	☐
15	☐	☐	☐	☐
16	☐	☐	☐	☐

How many children go to school by bike? _____
How many children go to school by bus? _____
How many children go to school by car? _____
How many children go to school on foot? _____

Green English - Level A   © Copyright ELI 2006

Worksheet 5.4

Water and Air

Date: _____
What's the weather like today? It's _____

Temperature
☐ Hot
☐ Warm
☐ Cold

Transport Record

Tick (✓) the means of transport you use this week.

Days	car	bike	walk	train	bus	other
MONDAY	☐	☐	☐	☐	☐	☐
TUESDAY	☐	☐	☐	☐	☐	☐
WEDNESDAY	☐	☐	☐	☐	☐	☐
THURSDAY	☐	☐	☐	☐	☐	☐
FRIDAY	☐	☐	☐	☐	☐	☐
SATURDAY	☐	☐	☐	☐	☐	☐
SUNDAY	☐	☐	☐	☐	☐	☐

Complete:

On Monday I went to school by _____ .
On Tuesday I _____ .
On Wednesday _____ .
On Thursday _____ .
On Friday _____ .
On Saturday _____ .
On Sunday _____ .

How often?

never   sometimes   usually   always

I **NEVER** go to school by _____ . I **USUALLY** go by _____ .

Green English - Level A   © Copyright ELI 2006   Worksheet 5.5

The Organic Kitchen Garden

Date: _____
What's the weather like today? It's _____

Temperature
☐ Hot
☐ Warm
☐ Cold

Organic Vegetables

✂ Cut outs: 🖍 paste the names of the vegetables.

Green English - Level A   © Copyright ELI 2006   Worksheet 6.1

The Organic Kitchen Garden

Date: _____
What's the weather like today? It's _____

Temperature
☐ Hot
☐ Warm
☐ Cold

Survey: What's your Favourite Vegetable?

My favourite vegetable is _____

	Name	Vegetable
1		
2		
3		
4		
5		
6		
7		
8		
9		
10		
11		
12		
13		
14		
15		
16		
17		
18		
19		
20		
21		
22		

The most popular vegetable is _____

Green English - Level A © Copyright ELI 2006

Worksheet 6.2

The Organic Kitchen Garden

Date: _____

What's the weather like today? It's _____

Temperature
- ☐ Hot
- ☐ Warm
- ☐ Cold

Song 🎧 This is the Way

✏️ **Draw the actions.**

This is the way we weed the garden,
weed the garden, weed the garden,
This is the way we weed the garden,
In the English kitchen garden.

This is the way we dig the ground,
Dig the ground, dig the ground,
This is the way we dig the ground,
In the English kitchen garden.

This is the way we plant the seeds,
Plant the seeds, plant the seeds,
This is the way we plant the seeds,
In the English kitchen garden.

This is the way we water our plants,
Water our plants, water our plants,
This is the way we water our plants,
In the English kitchen garden.

This is the way we feed our plants,
Feed our plants, feed our plants,
This is the way we feed our plants,
In the English kitchen garden.

This is the way our veggies will grow,
Veggies will grow, veggies will grow,
This is the way our veggies will grow,
In the English kitchen garden.

This is the way we eat them all,
Eat them all, eat them all,
This is the way we eat them all,
In the English kitchen garden.

Green English - Level A   © Copyright ELI 2006

Worksheet 6.3

The Organic Kitchen Garden

Date: _____
What's the weather like today? It's _____

Temperature
☐ Hot
☐ Warm
☐ Cold

In the Kitchen Garden

Vegetables	Is it in your kitchen garden? YES = ✓ NO = ✗	Which part do you eat? Tuber / Seeds / Leaves / Stem / Roots / Fruit / Flower / Bulb
artichoke		We eat the _____
courgette		_____
beans		_____
carrot		_____
cauliflower		_____
celery		_____
aubergine		_____
garlic		_____
lettuce		_____
onion		_____
peas		_____
potato		_____
sweet pepper		_____

Green English - Level A   © Copyright ELI 2006   Worksheet 6.4

The Pond

Date: _____
What's the weather like today? It's _____

Temperature
☐ Hot
☐ Warm
☐ Cold

In and around the Pond

Observe. What animals can you see in and around the pond?

- DRAGONFLY
- TURTLE
- ROCKS
- WORM
- GROUND
- FROG
- WATER LILY
- DUCK
- FISH
- AQUATIC PLANTS

Describe the picture.

Use the prepositions: IN   UNDER   ON   OVER   AROUND

The dragonfly is _in the air._ _____
The frog is _____ _____
The fish _____ _____
_____ _____
_____ _____
_____ _____

Green English - Level A © Copyright ELI 2006

Worksheet 7.1

The Pond

Date: _____
What's the weather like today? It's _____

Temperature
☐ Hot
☐ Warm
☐ Cold

Experiment: Let's Make a Mini-Pond

✏️ **Draw. You need:**

a plastic bowl	a plastic bag	soil
stones	plants, twigs for decoration	water

Instructions:

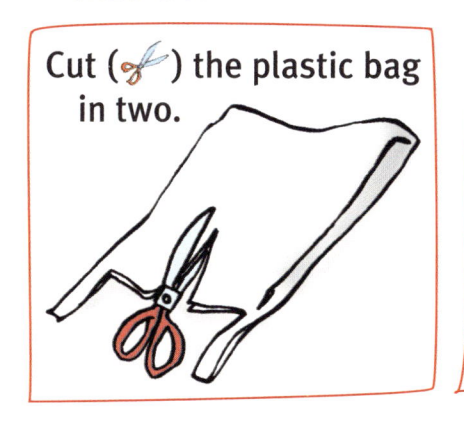

- Cut (✂) the plastic bag in two.
- Put a piece of plastic in the bowl.
- Fill the bowl with soil.
- Make a big hole in the soil.
- Cover the soil with the second piece of plastic.
- Put stones and soil all around.
- Decorate with plants, pebbles...
- Fill the pond with water.

Put your pond in your school garden!

Green English - Level A   © Copyright ELI 2006   Worksheet 7.2

The Pond

Date: _____
What's the weather like today? It's _____

Temperature
☐ Hot
☐ Warm
☐ Cold

Pond Record

Observe your pond. Write and/or draw what you can see.
Keywords: I can see … , I can't see … , There is … , There isn't … , There are some … , There aren't any … .

Date

Date

Date

Date

Date

Date

Date

Date

Green English - Level A   © Copyright ELI 2006

Worksheet 7.3

The Pond

Date: _____
What's the weather like today? It's _____

Temperature
☐ Hot
☐ Warm
☐ Cold

Game: Stepping Stones

✂ Cut outs: use the frogs and the cards to play the game.

Green English - Level A   © Copyright ELI 2006   Worksheet 7.4

The Pond

Date: _____
What's the weather like today? It's _____

Temperature
☐ Hot
☐ Warm
☐ Cold

Song 🎧 Five Little Speckled Frogs

Sing and clap your hands.

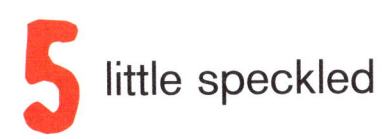

5 little speckled

Sitting on a speckled

Eating the most delicious    Yum, Yum **!**

1 jumps into the    where it is nice and cool,

Now there are

4 green speckled   •••

Green English - Level A   © Copyright ELI 2006   Worksheet 7.5

Bugs

Date: _____
What's the weather like today? It's _____

Temperature
☐ Hot
☐ Warm
☐ Cold

Bug Hunt

Find these bugs in your garden. YES = ✓ NO = ✗

☐ GRASSHOPPER

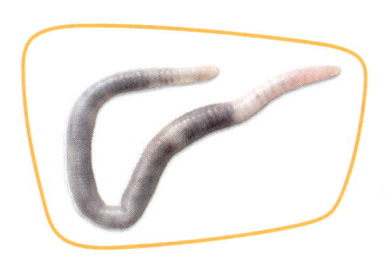

☐ WORM

☐ LADYBIRD

☐ BEE

☐ SPIDER

☐ SNAIL

☐ BUTTERFLY

☐ DRAGONFLY

☐ CATERPILLAR

☐ BEETLE

☐ ANT

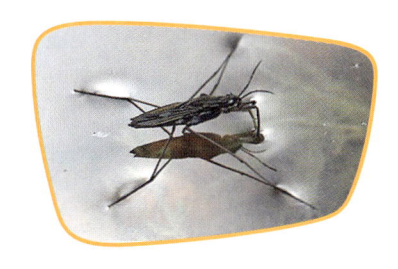

☐ POND SKATER

What can you see in your garden?

In my garden I can see _____

Green English - Level A   © Copyright ELI 2006

Worksheet 8.1

Bugs

Date: _____
What's the weather like today? It's _____

Temperature
- [ ] Hot
- [ ] Warm
- [ ] Cold

Make your Bug

✏️ **Draw. You need:**

a plastic bottle	cardboard
glue	sticky tape

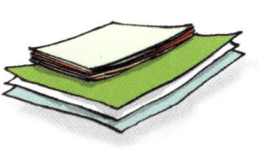

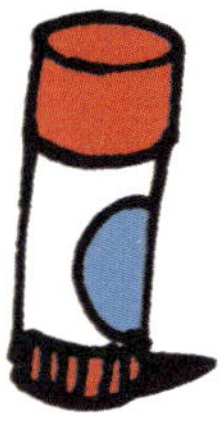

OTHER BITS AND PIECES

✏️ **Draw your favourite bug and label the picture. Use the Keywords:**
head , body , antennae , legs , eyes , mouth , wings , tail .

Green English - Level A   © Copyright ELI 2006

Worksheet 8.2

Bugs

Date: _____
What's the weather like today? It's _____

Temperature
☐ Hot
☐ Warm
☐ Cold

A Story 🎧 — Mr Caterpillar

Listen and mime.

1. Mr Caterpillar crawls.
2. Mr Caterpillar eats.
3. Mr Caterpillar works.
4. Mr Caterpillar sleeps.
5. Mr Caterpillar snores.
6. Mr Caterpillar's shy.
7. Where is Mr Caterpillar?
8. He's become a butterfly.

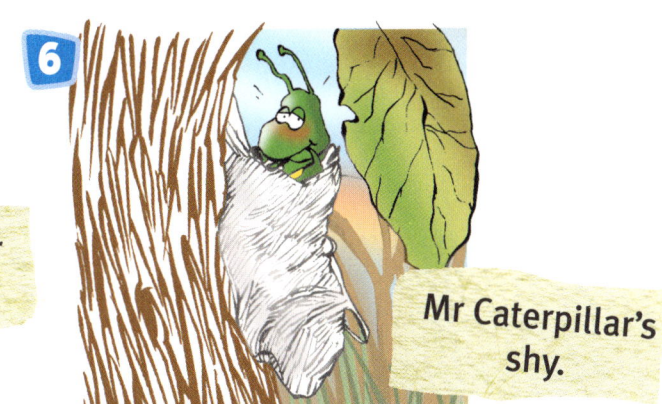

Green English - Level A   © Copyright ELI 2006   FACT FILES 7-8   Worksheet 8.3

Bugs

Date: _____
What's the weather like today? It's _____

Temperature
☐ Hot
☐ Warm
☐ Cold

Butterfly Life Cycle

egg → caterpillar → cocoon → butterfly

✏️ **Colour and write the numbers in the boxes.**

☐ The caterpillar eats some leaves.

☐ The caterpillar goes to sleep in a cocoon.

☐ The caterpillar wakes up and …

☐ …it's a beautiful butterfly!!!

☐ On a leaf in the garden there is a tiny egg.

☐ The egg goes "POP!!!". Out comes a tiny caterpillar.

Green English - Level A   © Copyright ELI 2006   FACT FILES 7-8   Worksheet 8.4

Bugs

Date: _____
What's the weather like today? It's _____

Temperature
- [ ] Hot
- [ ] Warm
- [ ] Cold

Experiment: How to Make a Wormery

✏️ Draw. You need:

a large jar	a plastic bottle	soil	sand	sticky tape
elastic band	leaves and grass for food		mesh	dark paper

Instructions:

- Cut (✂) a plastic bottle. 
- Put it in the jar.
- Add sand and soil in layers. 
- Wrap the dark paper round the jar. Fix it with sticky tape. 
- Add a few worms, grass and leaves for food.
- Cover the jar with the mesh. Fix with the elastic band.
- Leave the jar in a cool place for 2-3 days. 
- Take off the paper. What can you see?

✏️ Draw it here.

Green English - Level A   © Copyright ELI 2006

Worksheet 8.5

See, Smell, Touch

Date: _____
What's the weather like today? It's _____

Temperature
- [ ] Hot
- [ ] Warm
- [ ] Cold

See, Smell, Touch

Explore the garden. Draw and write.

I can see _____
_____

I can hear _____
_____

I can feel _____
_____

I can smell _____
_____

Green English - Level A © Copyright ELI 2006

Worksheet 9.1

See, Smell, Touch

Date: _____
What's the weather like today? It's _____

Temperature
- [ ] Hot
- [ ] Warm
- [ ] Cold

A Feely-box

You need:

a shoe box   scissors   objects

What can you put in your feely-box? ✏️ **Draw.**

**Put the objects in the feely-box.
Ask your friends: "What is it?"**

Things I guessed:
_____
_____
_____

Things I DID NOT guess:
_____
_____
_____

Green English - Level A   © Copyright ELI 2006

Worksheet 9.2

See, Smell, Touch

Date: _____
What's the weather like today? It's _____

Temperature
☐ Hot
☐ Warm
☐ Cold

Let's Make a Herb Potpourri

Smell and 🖉 draw. 😊 It's lovely 🙂 It's nice 😐 It's ok 😖 It's yucky

- BASIL
- MINT 
- SAGE 
- PARSLEY 
- LAVENDER 
- CAMOMILE 
- ROSEMARY 
- OREGANO 
- THYME 

🖉 Write the names of the herbs and make your potpourri.

2 cups of thyme
1 cup of rosemary
1 cup of lavender
1 cup of mint
1/4 cup of cloves
1/2 cup of basil

A piece of cloth 
A piece of ribbon

Green English - Level A   © Copyright ELI 2006   Worksheet 9.3

A House in the Country

Date: _____
What's the weather like today? It's _____

Temperature
☐ Hot
☐ Warm
☐ Cold

The Farmhouse

✂ Cut outs: 🖍 paste the pictures and complete the country house.

chimney
bathroom
bedroom
fireplace
stable
shed
kitchen
pig
well
cock
chicks
chicken
horse
cow
donkey
duck

Ask your friend.

What is there in the kitchen? There is _____

What is there in the bedroom? _____

Where is the duck? _____

Green English - Level A   © Copyright ELI 2006   Worksheet 10.1

A House in the Country

Date: _____
What's the weather like today? It's _____

Temperature
☐ Hot
☐ Warm
☐ Cold

Farm Animals

✂ Cut outs: 🖌 paste the words in the bubbles.
What do they do? Match.

COCK-A-DOODLE-DOO

They produce EGGS

They WORK HARD

They produce MILK

They WAKE US UP

They SMELL

They RUN FAST

They produce WOOL

They COME FROM EGGS

Green English - Level A © Copyright ELI 2006

Worksheet 10.2

A House in the Country

Date: _____

What's the weather like today? It's _____

Temperature
- [ ] Hot
- [ ] Warm
- [ ] Cold

Save Energy in your House

Spot the differences.

A

B

Choose the correct answer.

When you brush your teeth.	☐ tap on ☐ tap off
When the heating is on.	☐ windows open ☐ windows closed
When the room is empty.	☐ lights on ☐ lights off
When you throw rubbish away.	☐ one bin ☐ different bins

Green English - Level A   © Copyright ELI 2006

Worksheet 10.3

A House in the Country

Date: _____
What's the weather like today? It's _____

Temperature
☐ Hot
☐ Warm
☐ Cold

A Mobile for your Room

You need:

| two twigs |  string | 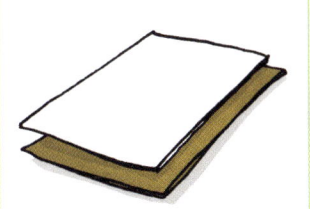 cardboard |  felt-tip |
| 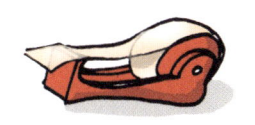 sticky tape |  scissors | 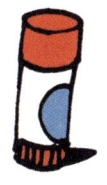 glue |  leaves |

✎ Write and draw.

My favourite flower is _____

My favourite leaf is _____

My favourite fruit is _____

My favourite bug is _____

Follow the instructions.

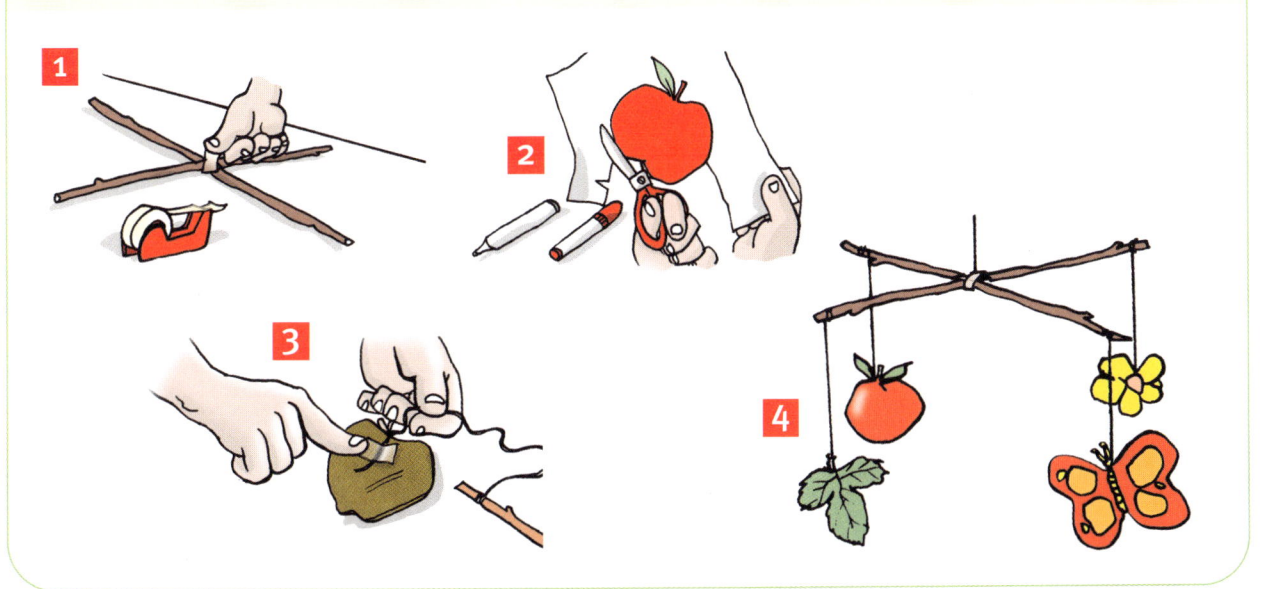

1
2
3
4

Green English - Level A   © Copyright ELI 2006

Worksheet 10.4

🌿 Green English – Cut Outs

Worksheet 1.3

RESPECT	BE SMART	RECYCLE
REDUCE	BE KIND	REUSE

1st 2nd 3rd 4th 5th 6th 7th

Worksheet 7.4

Worksheet 6.1

GAR	RAGUS	FLO	P	WER	NS	CHOKE
ROTS	LIC	ASPA	CAR	ERY		LET
KIN	TOES	ON	PER	AUBE		TUCE
ARTI	BEA	POTA	PUMP	CEL		COUR
GETTES	PEP	EAS	CAULI	RGINE		ONI

Worksheet 10.1

Worksheet 10.2

| HEE-HAW | CLUCK-CLUCK | MOO | BAA | NEIGH | OINK-OINK | CHEEP-CHEEP |

Worksheet 7.4

What colour is a frog?	What colour is a leaf?	What colour is water?	What's in a pond?
What's the name of a baby frog?	Name an animal that flies.	Name an animal that swims.	Name an animal that jumps.
How many waterlilies are there in the picture?	How many stones are there in the picture?	How many dragonflies are there in the picture?	How many butterflies are there in the picture?
Is bamboo a plant or an animal?	What is "pond" in your language?	What is "water" in your language?	What is "dragonfly" in your language?
Is there an elephant in the picture?	Is there a motorbike in the picture?	Is there a fish in the picture?	Is there a bee in the picture?

Green English – Mind Map

My Favourite Activities

- Welcome
- The Orchard
- Plants
- The Three R's
- Water and Air
- The Organic Kitchen Garden
- The Pond
- Bugs
- See, Smell, Touch
- A House in the Country

Green English
Environmental Education

Green English A – Index

Topics	Worksheets
1 Welcome	1.1 Green English Kids 1.2 Our Green English Logo 1.3 Green English Keywords
2 The Orchard	2.1 Parts of a Tree 2.2 My First Tree 2.3 Seasons 2.4 Fruit 2.5 Survey: What's your Favourite Fruit?
3 Plants	3.1 Experiment: Growing Things 3.2 Experiment: What do Plants Need? 3.3 Leaf Rubbing 3.4 Leaf Classification
4 The Three R's	4.1 Survey (1): What do you Recycle? 4.2 Survey (2): How much do you Recycle? 4.3 Rubbish Bins 4.4 Reuse: Let's Make a Puppet! 4.5 Make your own Paper
5 Water and Air	5.1 Experiment: Soluble/Insoluble 5.2 Experiment: Does it Float? 5.3 A Story: Drip the Drop 5.4 Survey: How do you Go to school? 5.5 Transport Record

Green English A – Index

Topics	Worksheets
6 The Organic Kitchen Garden	6.1 Organic Vegetables 6.2 Survey: What's your Favourite Vegetable? 6.3 Song: This is the Way 6.4 In the Kitchen Garden
7 The Pond	7.1 In and around the Pond 7.2 Experiment: Let's Make a Mini-pond 7.3 Pond Record 7.4 Game: Stepping Stones 7.5 Song: Five Little Speckled Frogs
8 Bugs	8.1 Bug Hunt 8.2 Make your Bug 8.3 A story: Mr Caterpillar 8.4 Butterfly Life Cycle 8.5 How to Make a Wormery
9 See, Smell, Touch	9.1 See, Smell, Touch 9.2 A Feely-box 9.3 Let's Make a Herb Potpourri
10 A House in the Country	10.1 The Farmhouse 10.2 Farm Animals 10.3 Save Energy in your House 10.4 A Mobile for your Room

Cut-outs
Certificate
Mind Map

© 2006 – ELI s.r.l.
P.O. Box 6 – 62019 Recanati – Italy
Tel.: +39 071 750701 – Fax: +39 071 977851
www.elionline.com
e-mail: info@elionline.com

HandsOnLanguage
Green English
by Damiana Covre and Melanie Segal

Graphic design by Studio Cornell sas
Illustrated by Roberto Battistini

This book is sold subject to the condition that it shall not,
by way of trade or otherwise, be lent, resold, hired out,
or otherwise circulated without the publisher's prior consent
in any form of binding or cover other than that in which it is published
and without a similar condition including this condition
being imposed on the subsequent purchaser.

Printed in Italy by Tecnostampa – 06.83.189.0

| ISBN 10 | 88-536-1028-X | Green English - Worksheet A |
| ISBN 13 | 9788853610287 | |

| ISBN 10 | 88-536-1029-8 | Green English - Worksheet B |
| ISBN 13 | 9788853610294 | |

| ISBN 10 | 88-536-1030-1 | Green English - Special Guide + Audio CD |
| ISBN 13 | 9788853610300 | |